Introduction

Planning social studies lessons for my fourth graders always proved challenging for me: Not only were there myriad skills to teach—from using a compass rose to finding information in nonfiction sources—there was also a tremendous amount of content to cover—from the Texas history curriculum to the background students needed to understand other cultures and histories for school-wide learning units such as Black History Month.

Many of my students thrived on creating visual and spatial representations of information they had read or heard. Graphic organizers became a useful tool for showing information they had read on a map, taking notes from the social studies textbook, and even organizing their oral presentations. The graphic organizers in this collection are designed to meet a range of learning objectives in social studies, including building skills, understanding key concepts, understanding social studies texts, and conducting research. Some of these organizers have been adapted from traditional organizers, like K-W-L charts, and some were inspired by the specific learning objectives with which my students needed help.

What Is a Graphic Organizer?

A graphic organizer is a visual and graphic representation of relationships among ideas and concepts. This instructional tool comes in a variety of formats—from loose webs to structured grids—that help students process information they've gathered and organize their ideas. We generally design graphic organizers to follow one of four patterns of knowledge: hierarchical, conceptual, sequential, and cyclical (Bromley et al., 1995).

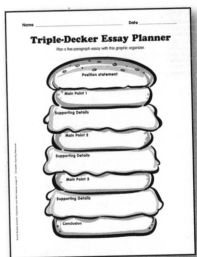

Hierarchical organizers use principles of rank and order to help students break down a concept. These organizers make excellent study aids and scaffolds for writing assignments. For example, the "Triple-Decker Essay Planner" (page 36) offers a hierarchical structure that helps students move systematically from one level of information to the next as they organize their persuasive writing ideas—from a central statement of opinion to convincing arguments, and then to supporting details for each argument.

Conceptual organizers, such as webs, provide a format for enumerating the attributes of the main topic or idea. The nonlinear, open-ended structure assists students in generating ideas for a topic in the early stages of research. The "Cause-Effect Blossom" (page 16) is an example of a conceptual organizer characterized by a central space for recording an important historical event and radiating spaces in which students can list multiple causes or effects for that event.

Sequential organizers are used to show time-order relationships. Often linear in format, they can help students link causes and effects, sort chronological events, and identify problem-solution relationships. A good example of this format is "Up-the-Stairs Time Line" (page 12) in which students write key events, in chronological order, leading up to a major historical event or turning point.

Cyclical organizers are used to show an ordered series of events that are part of a repeating pattern. The circular structure of these graphic organizers helps students present, in order, each element in a series, cycle, or succession. For example, the circular pattern presented in "Winds of Change" (page 22) offers a way to show a continuous sequence of steps in legislative processes, such as passing a bill or electing a government official.

Why Use Graphic Organizers?

Graphic organizers make teaching and learning rewarding. Visually appealing and accessible to both struggling and advanced students, graphic organizers help students to:

- connect prior knowledge to new information (Guastello, 2000);
- integrate language and thinking in an organized format (Bromley et al., 1995);
- increase comprehension and retention of text (Boyle & Weishaar, 1997; Chang, K. et al, 2002; Moore & Readence, 1984);
- organize writing (Ellis, 1994);
- engage in mid- to high levels of thinking along Bloom's Taxonomy (application, analysis, evaluation, and synthesis) (Dodge, 2005).

One factor influencing the effectiveness of graphic organizers is the instructional context in which they are used. Studies suggest that to maximize the impact of graphic organizers on student learning, teachers need to state the purpose for using the organizer, model how to use it, and provide students with multiple opportunities for guided and independent practice and feedback.

(National Center on Accessing the General Curriculum, 2002)

How Are the Organizers Arranged in This Book?

The 20 graphic organizers in this book are grouped in three sections: Social Studies Skills/Concepts, Reading and Writing in Social Studies, and Research & Presentations. In the first section, you'll find organizers geared to the key skills and concepts in social studies that students need to master, such as ordering chronological events, evaluating primary sources, reading a map, and making historical and cultural comparisons. In the second section, the organizers are designed to help students better navigate and comprehend historical fiction and nonfiction texts and to write clear summaries of these texts as well as their own essays or reports on historical subjects. In the final section, organizers scaffold student work as they develop research questions, gather and evaluate their sources, and prepare effective oral presentations.

SCHOLASTIC

Social Studies
Graphic Organizers
& Mini-Lessons

by Sarah Longhi

NEW YORK • TORONTO • LONDON • AUCKLAND • SYDNEY
MEXICO CITY • NEW DELHI • HONG KONG • BUENOS AIRES

Teaching
Resources

Dedication

For the students and staff at Garcia Elementary—you've taught me so much.

Acknowledgments

A special thank you to both my editor, Maria Chang, for her patience, humor, and great problem-solving skills, and to my husband, Brian, for his support and faith in me.

Cover design by Maria Lilja
Interior design by Jeffrey Dorman
Illustrations by Dave Clegg

ISBN 0-439-54894-2
Copyright © 2006 by Sarah Longhi
All rights reserved.
Printed in the USA.

3 4 5 6 7 8 9 10   40   12 11 10 09 08 07

Contents

CL
Al

SOCIAL STUDIES GRAPHIC ORGANIZERS & MINI-LESSONS

Using the Lessons and Graphic Organizers in This Book

The organizers can be used flexibly for a variety of learning situations for students in grades 4–6: whole class, small groups, and individuals. Use them as motivational graphic aids to teach and practice skills and concepts, or use them as resources to support students in reading, writing, and researching.

Each lesson includes a skills focus, a statement of purpose, teaching suggestions, student samples, and a reproducible graphic organizer.

You can implement the organizers in any of the following ways:

- Draw the organizer on the board or on chart paper.
- Use the organizer as a template for an overhead transparency.
- Reproduce multiple copies of the organizer to pass out to students during class work.
- Have copies of the organizer available for students to use while reading and working independently.

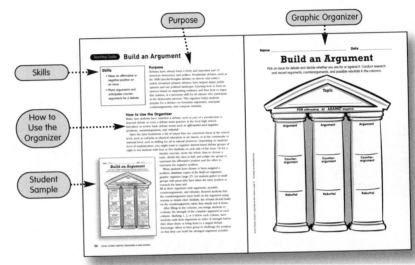

For whole-class instruction, use the lessons and the graphic organizers to model how to organize information visually. Invite students to offer ideas and suggest where this information would go in the organizer; this helps build background for their independent or small-group work.

For small-group instruction, use the lessons and graphic organizers to provide students with the opportunity to work and learn cooperatively. When students are familiar with the format and purpose of an organizer, you can adapt it for use as a game or group activity. As students build background and brainstorm together, their learning is enriched by one another's experiences.

For independent learning, use the graphic organizers to keep students engaged and focused on learning objectives. Once you've demonstrated how to complete the organizer, provide students with copies of the reproducible so they may complete their own during independent work time.

K-W-L-S Chart

Skills

- Identifies prior knowledge about a unit of study
- Sets learning goals for a unit of study

Purpose

The traditional KWL (What I **K**now, What I **W**ant to Know, What I **L**earned) chart helps students build schema (background knowledge) about a particular topic or unit of study. The added category in the KWLS version helps students reflect on the information they've gathered: In space "**S**" they show what they *still* want to learn.

How to Use the Organizer

This flexible organizer can be adapted to any social studies subject. An effective way to use this organizer is to create an interactive class chart that you keep posted throughout a unit of study. Enlarge the K-W-L-S graphic organizer (page 9) to poster-size on a copier, or draw a large version on chart paper. Tape the chart to a wall so you and your class can frequently access it to record new information.

When you introduce the unit of study, ask students what they already know about the topic and record the information in the "K" column. Explain that the class will revisit this information as everyone learns more about the topic.

Encourage students to share information about the unit of study, and invite them to generate questions they want to research further. Record their questions in the "W" column.

As the class researches and locates information that addresses their questions, write (or have students write) the new information in the "L" column. Remind students to revise their K-column statements as they find more accurate information.

Finally, in the middle or toward the end of the unit, revisit the chart as a class and have students generate questions about what they still want to know. Record the questions in the "S" space. At the end of the unit, students may want to write their answers on a new sheet of chart paper or simply share the information at a group meeting. The cycle of revisiting old knowledge, recording new information, and asking questions helps students practice research as an ongoing process of learning.

More to Do

To differentiate the activity, have each student use the K-W-L-S Chart to track his or her learning before, during, and after a unit of study.

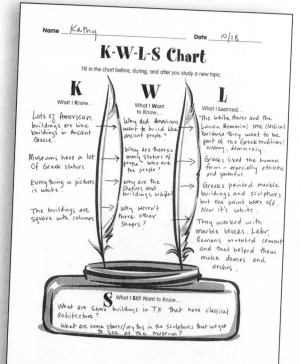

K-W-L-S Chart

Fill in the chart before, during, and after you study a new topic.

K
What I **K**now...

W
What I **W**ant
to Know...

L
What I **L**earned...

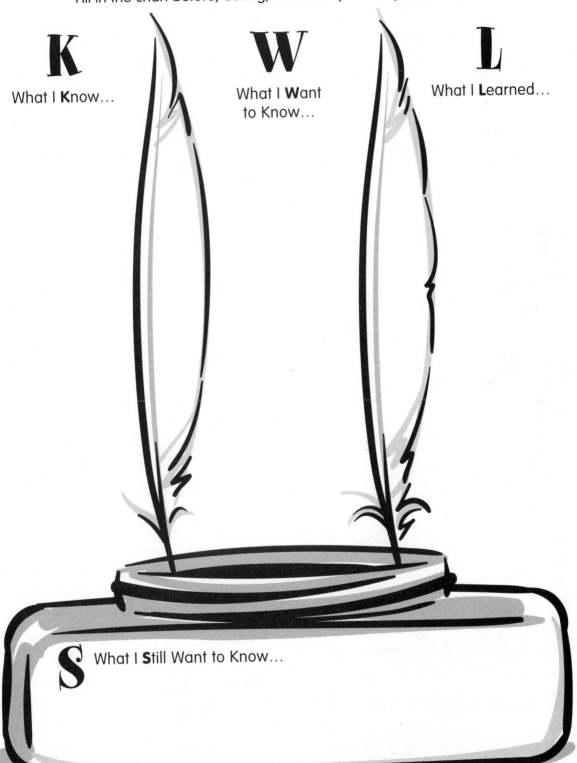

S What I **S**till Want to Know...

On the Clock

Skills

- Organizes information about the daily life of a historical figure or group
- Represents the sequence of a specific historical event using a chronological framework

Purpose

By mapping out a structure of daily life from a historical period using a clock format, students work from a familiar place—their own daily timeframe. Recording the details of a day in the life of a historical figure, such as Hatshepsut, or of a person representing a specific historical group, such as a blacksmith's apprentice in Massachusetts Colony, gives students a window of insight into a different way of life and a clearer understanding of the environmental and cultural influences of life in a particular historical period.

How to Use the Organizer

Use this organizer following a real or virtual field trip to a historic place, such as colonial Williamsburg, or in conjunction with a real or fictional historical narrative, such as one of the Dear America series.

Distribute to each student two copies of the On the Clock graphic organizer (page 11). Let students use the first copy to work individually or in groups to show a typical school day in the life of a boy or girl their age. Provide tips on creating the organizer, such as drawing lines from the center point to two numbers on the circumference and noting AM or PM to define a period of time. Ask students to share their organizers and the strategies they used to fill in the clock to show a school day.

Then discuss how a day in the life of a boy or girl (or specific person) from the historical period you're studying might look different. Have students choose their subject and fill in a new clock organizer. Encourage them to use reference materials or notes, or work from what they remember.

More to Do

For a more challenging approach to the organizer, have each student select an important historical event that took place over the course of 12 to 24 hours and fill in one or two copies of the clock organizer. Or place students in groups and distribute two copies of the organizer to each group. Have each group choose a different day in a series of events, such as the days leading up to and culminating in the battle of the Alamo. Let students work as a group to fill in the clock organizers to show the events in their chosen day. Then set the organizers in chronological order on a bulletin board for students' reference.

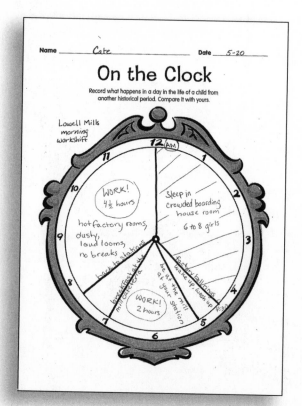

On the Clock

Divide the clock to record what happened in a day in history.

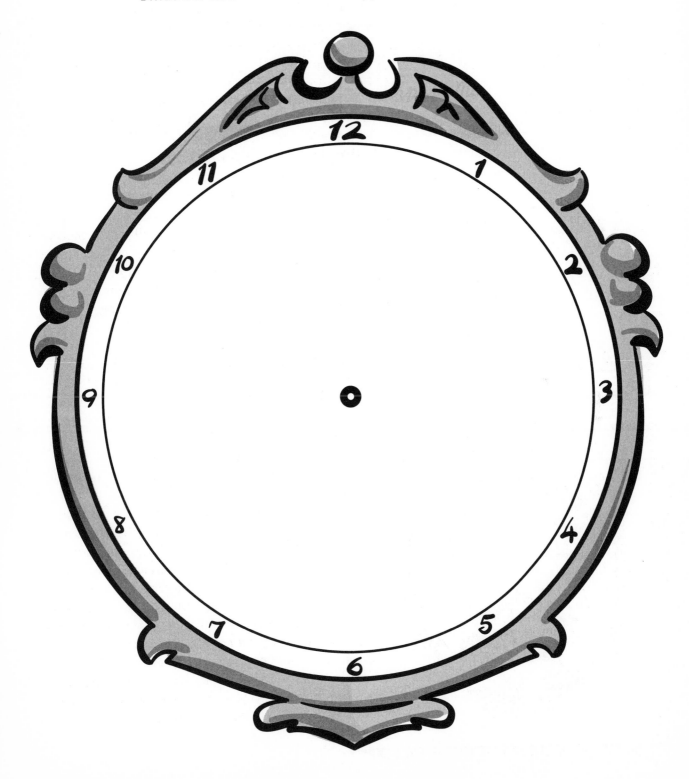

Up-the-Stairs Time Line

Skills

- Identifies and summarizes key events

- Selects an initiating and culminating event

- Sequences events chronologically

Purpose

Selecting a topic and culminating event, such as the beginning of World War II and Nazi Germany's invasion of Poland, is a helpful starting point for identifying a chain of events that led up to the culminating event. This organizer offers a structure in which students can organize information about a sequence of related events.

How to Use the Organizer

Lead a class discussion about the way events can build on one another and finally lead to a big end result. Like steps in a staircase rising to a new level, each event in a sequence moves closer and closer to a final (culminating) event.

Display a transparency copy of the Up-the-Stairs Time Line graphic organizer (page 13) on the overhead projector. Guide students as needed to select a topic and final event and to identify the key events leading up to the final event. For example, you might choose a final event such as the signing of the Declaration of Independence from your current unit of study on the American Revolution, and with student participation, complete the organizer on the overhead.

When students use the organizer independently, level the activity appropriately. Let students who need more support use a smaller section of the stairs so that they work with only two or three events. Have them write the date on each step, draw a symbol for the event in the picture frame, and write a phrase describing the event under the step.

Let students who need a challenge work with a longer series of events. Have them copy the organizer onto a larger sheet of paper and add more steps to the staircase. In the spaces under the steps they might add detailed notes about the events and list in the picture frames important people involved in the event.

More to Do

To show events both leading up to and following a major event, have students add a down-the-stairs time line to their up-the-stairs organizer by tracing the ascending stair pattern in reverse from the top stair. This reverse organizer may help students track social, political, or other changes that have occurred as a result of the culminating event.

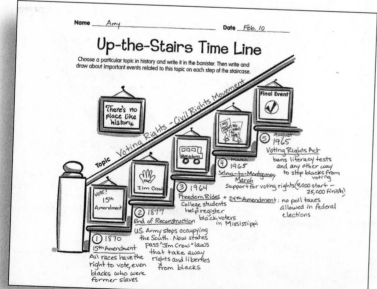

Name _____

Up-the-Stairs Time Line

Choose a particular topic in history and write it on the banister. Then write and
draw about important events related to this topic on each step of the staircase.

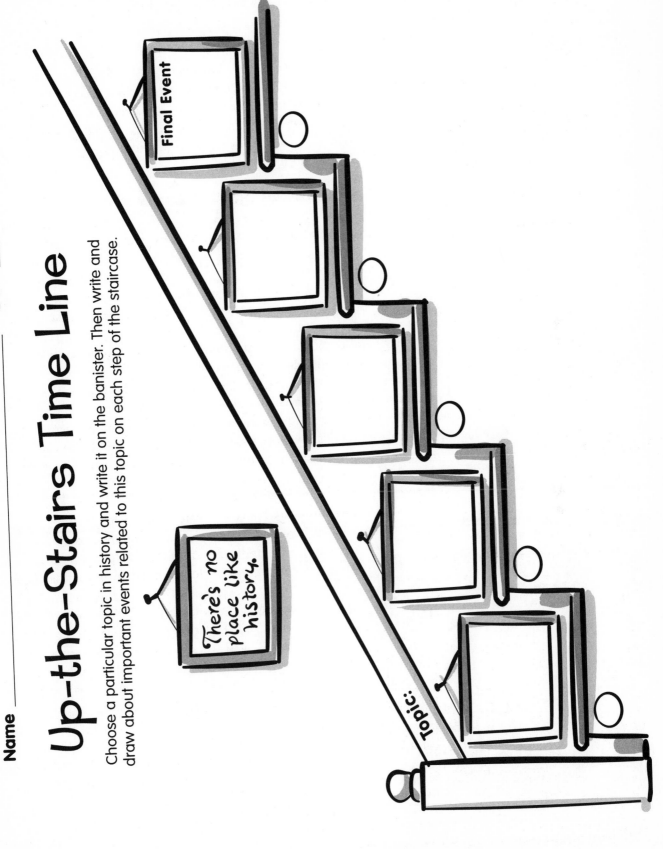

Final Event

There's no place like history.

Topic:

Paired Time Lines

Skills

- Identifies key events in history

- Sequences events chronologically

- Uses a scale to show the temporal distance between events

- Compares synchronistic events

Purpose

Time lines make helpful reference tools for organizing the sequence of important events in a given time period. Paired time lines also offer a way for students to represent two series of events within the same time period and use the scale of the time line to show the temporal distance between events along each time line.

How to Use the Organizer

Make sure students understand how to create a scale for a time line: Have them turn a piece of notebook paper horizontally and draw four parallel lines with more than an inch of space between them. (These lines intersect the printed lines of the notebook page to create a time line with date marks at evenly-spaced intervals.) Post on the chalkboard four sets of dates—one with dates over the course of several months, one with dates over the course of several decades, one with dates over the course of several years, and one with dates over the course of several centuries. Have students work individually or in groups to label each of the four time lines (by months, years, decades, and centuries respectively). Show solutions on the board for each time line with scales that fit all the given dates. Check that students are able to identify where specific events fall between the intervals (e.g., 1975 will fall exactly between the decade marks 1970 and 1980).

Once students can create a scale for a time line, have them identify a series of events occurring during the same time period for two different cultures (for example, technological advances during the Industrial Revolution in Europe and America) or for two different dimensions of the same culture (for example, events and advances in politics and science in Golden Age Greece).

Distribute copies of the Paired Time Line graphic organizer (page 15) and have students work individually or in pairs to select a scale for the time lines and place the selected events along the time line. They may want to use a different-colored pen to fill in each time line for visual contrast.

More to Do

Expand the organizers to include more events by trimming and taping another copy of the organizer onto the original. The time lines can also be enlarged to run along one or several walls, making a whole-class study aid.

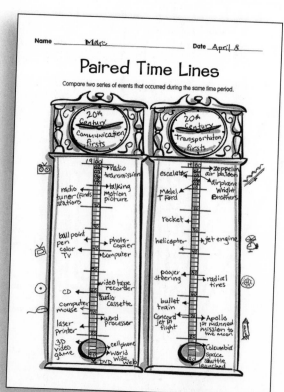

Paired Time Lines

Compare two series of events that occurred during the same time period.

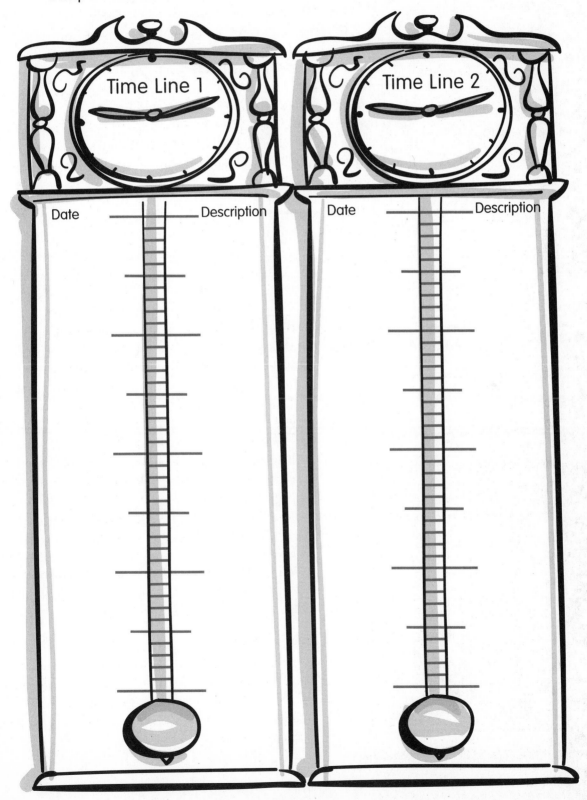

Cause-Effect Blossom

Skills

- Identifies a key cause or effect for an event
- Lists multiple effects or causes for the event

Purpose

No event can be linked to a single cause. Conversely, all events produce more than a single effect. This organizer helps students recognize that there are likely multiple results (effects) and causes for the important events they study.

How to Use the Organizer

If students are unfamiliar with cause-effect relationships, you might introduce related causes and effects with examples from the classroom (cause: you broke your only pencil tip before math class; effect: you sharpen the pencil when you get to class). Draw a simple graphic organizer on the board—an arrow pointing to a box. Write the cause in the stem of the arrow and the effect in the box.

Viviana started the race with her shoelace untied. → *She tripped and skinned her knee.*

When you want students to identify causes or effects for a current or historical event, have them research the event using several different sources. Distribute copies of the Cause-Effect Blossom graphic organizer (page 17). Let students fill in the center with the key event. Have them describe the related effects (or causes) in the radiating petals and circle the appropriate label (cause or effect).

To highlight the cause-effect relationship, have students trace an arrowhead on the dotted lines so that the arrow either points toward the center (showing an event with multiple causes) or out from the center (showing an event with multiple effects).

More to Do

Encourage students to draw a simple version of this organizer (e.g., a hexagon or circle with lines radiating out) when they take notes from a textbook or other source.

Name Ellen   Date 09/15

Cause-Effect Blossom

In the flower's center, record a key event in history that either triggered a series of events or was the result of different causes. Trace the arrow to show whether the surrounding events caused the central event or the central event caused the surrounding events.

Cause or Effect

Opens up "Great American Desert" to new farming families ⊕

Buffalo killed off in many areas (shot for sport) ⊖

Native American lands split up ⊖

Causes or Effects
Building of the Transcontinental Railroad ***** 1865 *****

Many killed b/c their food supply was gone ⊖

Faster travel across the country; by wagon: 5 months $1000 by train: 3 days $150 ⊕

100's of workers killed building the RR—dynamite explosions, freezing cold in the mountains, avalanches ⊖

Cause or Effect

Cause-Effect Blossom

In the flower's center, record a key event in history.
Write causes or effects of the events in the petals around it.

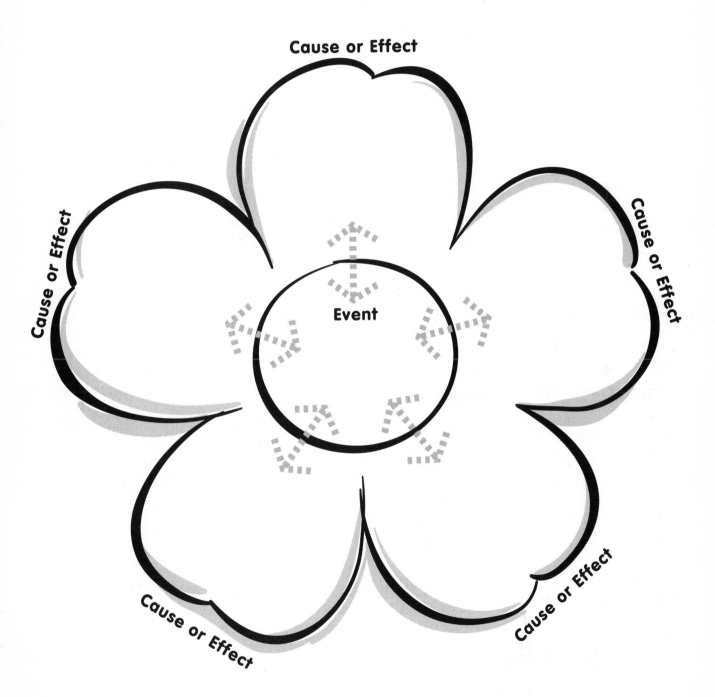

Cause or Effect

Cause or Effect

Cause or Effect

Event

Cause or Effect

Cause or Effect

Résumé Builder

Skills

- Collects biographical information about a historical figure

- Organizes biographical information into categories

- Organizes biographical details chronologically

Purpose

The first step toward structuring a biographical report or presentation is to select key details about the life and accomplishments of a historical or contemporary figure—without getting bogged down by interesting but extraneous details. As students synthesize information from their reading in the organizer, they eliminate unnecessary details and set in chronological order information about the accomplishments and events in the life of their subject.

How to Use the Organizer

You may want to introduce this organizer by showing students your own résumé or (with permission) the résumé of another professional. Discuss the function of a résumé: to present a concise record of a person's experiences and credentials to a potential employer by a) selecting only those details related to the job for which the person is applying and b) organizing the entries in each section from most to least recent.

When students have selected the figure they wish to study, distribute copies of the Résumé Builder graphic organizer (page 19). Review each section of the organizer with the class, comparing and contrasting the organizer to the professional résumé they have just read. Make sure to note that the Motto/Purpose section is like an objective section on a professional résumé—it will sum up what the person aims to accomplish. Ask students what the person they are studying might have said about his or her purpose or goal. For example, someone studying a president might use a campaign slogan or a memorable quotation, such as John F. Kennedy's "Ask not what your country can do for you, but what you can do for your country."

More to Do

Have students or groups use their completed organizers to structure a presentation or report. A presentation might be done in the form of a job interview. For example, a group of students representing the people of the United States of America might hold an interview for a presidential candidate and use the organizer categories to ask questions, such as how the candidate's work experiences have prepared him or her to lead the country. Another student playing the part of the candidate can use his or her group's responses on the organizer to generate answers.

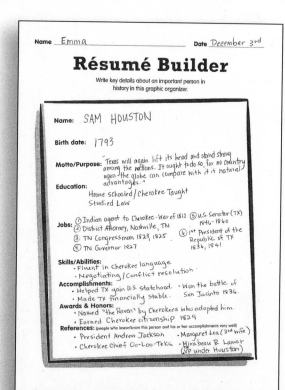

Résumé Builder

Write key details about an important person in
history in this graphic organizer.

Name:

Birth Date:

Motto/Purpose:

Education:

Jobs:

Skills/Abilities:

Accomplishments:

Awards & Honors:

References: (people who knew/know this person and his or her accomplishments very well)

Compare-Contrast Profiles

Skills

- Researches two historical or contemporary figures or groups

- Shows similarities and differences between these two subjects

Purpose

We can help students better understand a subject we're studying by having them compare that subject with another to identify similarities and differences. A version of the Venn diagram, this compare-contrast organizer helps students make comparisons at a biographical level between historical or contemporary figures, or at a broad cultural level between groups of people, types of governments, or religions.

How to Use the Organizer

Assign or have students choose two subjects to compare that will help them better understand the unit of study. For example, in a study of colonial America, the Compare-Contrast Profiles graphic organizer (page 21) can be used to compare two figures, such as two opposing leaders (Generals Washington and Cornwallis), two groups of people (French and British settlers), two religions or branches of a religion (Puritanism and Protestantism), or two types of government (democracy and monarchy). Make sure resources are available for students to research the two subjects and make the chosen comparisons.

Help students get started by brainstorming some categories by which to compare their subjects. Then distribute copies of the graphic organizer. Have students label the profiles on the organizer, writing one subject name at the top of each profile.

Tell students to record differences between the subjects in the appropriate profile, using the spaces that do not overlap. Have them record similarities between the subjects in the overlapping space.

When students compare two figures, you may want to refer students to the categories on the Résumé Builder graphic organizer on page 19. For students who need more support, have them first work in small groups or pairs to complete résumé organizers for two different figures, and then have them complete this compare-contrast organizer using the biographical information they have collected.

Name Candice   Date 08/16

Compare-Contrast Profiles

Compare two important people in history with this Venn diagram.

Compare-Contrast Profiles

Compare two important people in history with this Venn diagram.

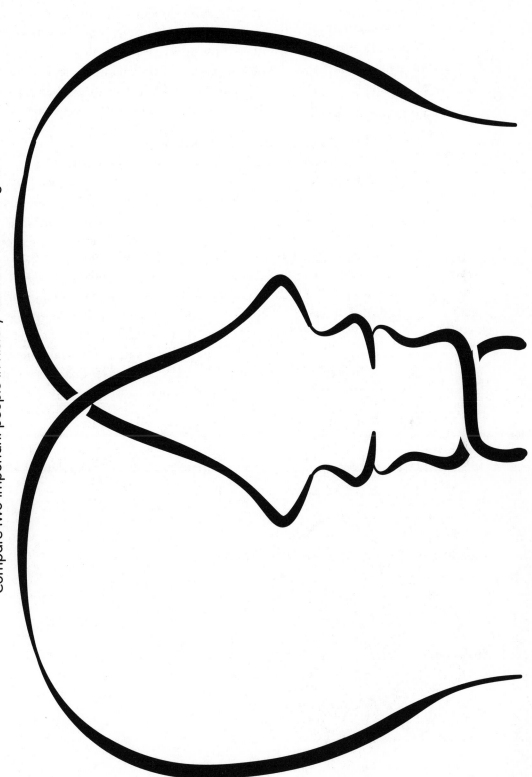

Winds of Change

Skills

• Tracks the steps of a cyclical process, such as passing a law or electing a public official

Purpose

A democratic system of government relies on a system of checks and balances that often occurs in a cyclical rather than a linear process. This organizer helps students break down a political or legislative process and track its progress. As they complete the organizer, they discover that each time the cycle completes itself, it begins again.

How to Use the Organizer

Select a cyclical process for students to learn about, such as passing a law or electing a government official. Provide students with several sources to help them identify the steps in the process. (A reliable and entertaining source for information on passing a law is School House Rock's musical animated short "I'm Just a Bill," available now in VHS format and reprinted on the Web at www.school-house-rock.com/Bill.html.)

Once students have collected the information they need and understand the process, distribute copies of the Winds of Change graphic organizer (page 23). Have students select the number of steps to include in the organizer, number the circles, and fill in the spaces with information. Show students how to draw an arrow from one area of the cycle to another to note when a particular step in the cycle is repeated, such as a bill being sent back from the Senate to the House of Representatives for revision.

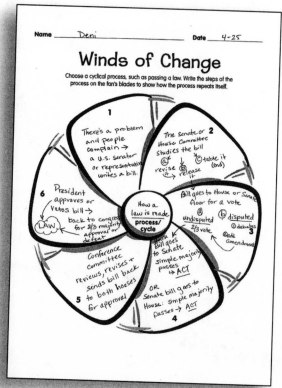

More to Do

To create a simpler organizer with three steps, make a copy of page 23 and use correction fluid to erase the lines dividing every other space. Then connect the lines at the tops to make three large fan-blade shapes in the cycle. To add complexity to the organizer, draw lines to divide the blade shapes in half. This will allow students to fill in up to twelve steps in a cycle.

Name ______________________________ Date ______________

Winds of Change

Choose a cyclical process, such as passing a law. Write the steps of the process on the fan's blades to show how the process repeats itself.

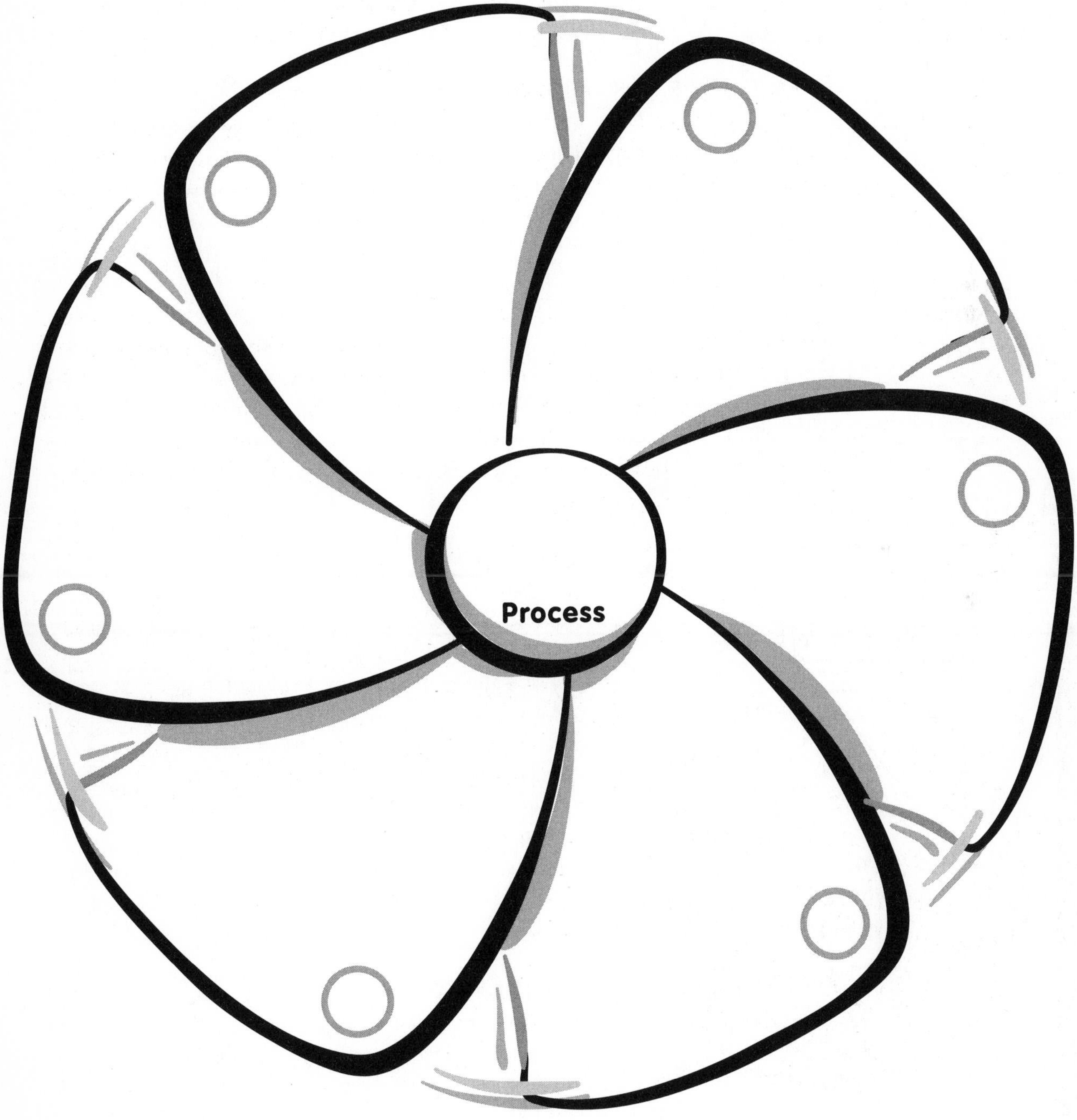

Map-a-Way

Skills

- Uses cardinal and ordinal directions to find information on a map or globe

- Reads different types of maps

Purpose

This organizer helps students explore any map oriented along north-south-east-west axes. Using directions to navigate their way around the map, students can compare elements such as elevation levels or population density in different areas of the same map or identify elements relative to a given position.

How to Use the Organizer

Select the type of map you want students to explore (a globe or any type of map with a compass rose will do). Have students work individually or in pairs. Make sure each individual or pair has access to the map in a social studies textbook, in an atlas or other reference book, or online.

Review cardinal and ordinal directions with the class by having students start with one hand at the center of the map. Call out each direction and have them quickly place their hands on the correct area of the map.

When students are ready to explore the map on their own or in pairs, distribute copies of the Map-a-Way graphic organizer (page 25). Have them write the map title and type of map in the center of the page. To keep the lesson basic or to introduce a new type of map, have students record "center" on the line labeled "Reference Point." Then, starting at the center of the map, have students search the map like detectives, looking in each of the cardinal directions for all the elements they can find or for all instances of a specific kind of element, such as mountain ranges on a topographical map. Students should record their findings in the space on the organizer that matches the direction in which they've searched.

For a more challenging exploration, have students use cardinal and ordinal directions relative to a specific point on the map. Assign or ask students to choose a position on the map (using latitude and longitude coordinates or a landmark) and record it on the organizer on the line labeled "Reference Point." In each of the direction spaces on the organizer have students record the elements (or a specific type of element) they've found relative to their reference point.

More to Do

Use the completed organizers to lead a class discussion about map elements specific to a particular type of map or to compare elements in different areas of the same map, such as elevation levels in east and west Texas.

Name _____ **Date** _____

Map-a-Way

Explore a map with this organizer and record your
findings on the appropriate compass points.

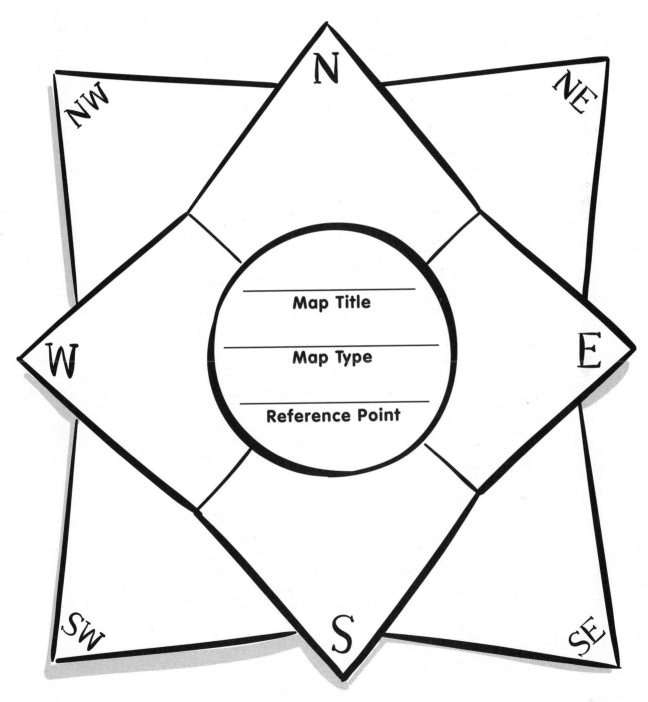

Build an Argument

Skills

- Takes an affirmative or negative position on an issue

- Plans arguments and anticipates counter-arguments for a debate

Purpose

Debates have always been a lively and important part of American democracy and politics. Presidential debates, such as the 1858 Lincoln-Douglas debates on slavery and today's widely broadcast primary debates, have helped shape public opinion and our political landscape. Learning how to form an opinion based on supporting evidence, and then how to argue that opinion, is a necessary skill for all citizens who participate in the democratic process. This organizer helps students prepare for a debate—to formulate arguments, anticipate counterarguments, and compose rebuttals.

How to Use the Organizer

Make sure students have watched a debate, such as part of a presidential or mayoral debate or even a debate team practice at the local high school. Introduce or review basic debate terms such as *affirmative and negative positions, counterargument*, and *rebuttal*.

Have the class brainstorm a list of issues they are concerned about at the school level, such as cutbacks in physical education or art classes, or at the community or national level, such as drilling for oil in natural preserves. Depending on students' level of sophistication, you might want to organize interest-based debate groups of eight to ten students with four or five students on each side of the issue. Or for a simpler exercise, invite the whole class to choose a topic, divide the class in half, and assign one group to represent the affirmative position and the other to represent the negative position.

When students have chosen or been assigned a position, distribute copies of the Build an Argument graphic organizer (page 27). Let students gather in small groups with peers who have taken the same position to research the issue and fill in their organizers with arguments, possible counterarguments, and rebuttals. Remind students that the counterargument must build on the argument using reasons or details cited. Similarly, the rebuttal should build on the counterargument, rather than simply tear it down.

After filling in the columns, encourage students to evaluate the strength of the complete argument in each column. Marking 1, 2, or 3 below each column, have students rank their arguments in order of strength before they share them or bring them to a staged debate. Encourage others in their group to challenge the position so that they can build the strongest argument possible.

Build an Argument

Pick an issue for debate and decide whether you are for or against it. Conduct research and record arguments, counterarguments, and possible rebuttals in the columns.

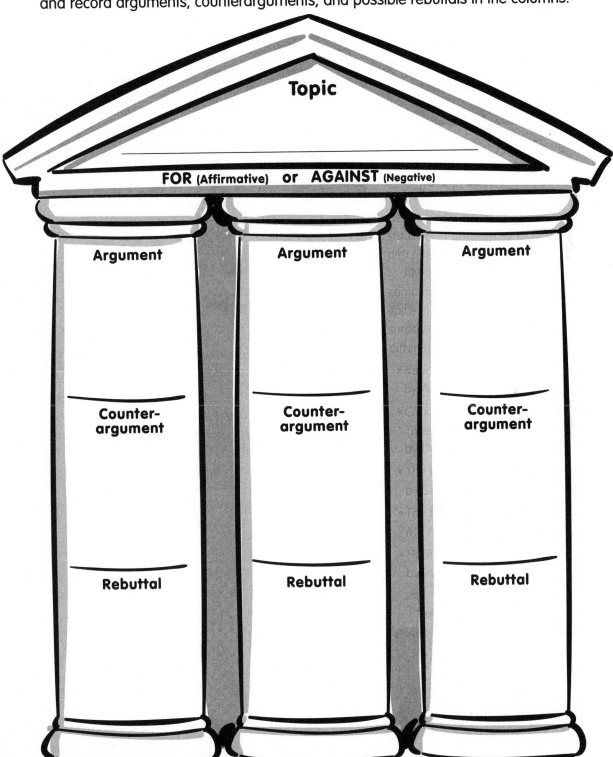

Topic

_____

FOR (Affirmative)   or   AGAINST (Negative)

Argument	Argument	Argument
Counter-argument	Counter-argument	Counter-argument
Rebuttal	Rebuttal	Rebuttal

Primary Source Close-Up

Skills/Standards

- Identifies features of a primary source

- Accurately describes the presentation of a subject

- Analyzes the presentation and purposes the document may have served

Purpose

A close study of primary sources (original photographs, newspaper articles, diaries, speeches, and so on) reveals details specific to time, place, culture, and viewpoint. Primary sources offer a window into history that cannot be replicated by a textbook passage or other secondary source.

This organizer helps students carefully describe what is being presented in a primary source document and focus on various elements of the document that will help them make critical judgments about its dependability and usefulness.

How to Use the Organizer

Select a primary source document to share with the class. (The Library of Congress "American Memory" Web site at http://memory.loc.gov/ammem offers many primary sources that can supplement your American history curriculum.) Make photocopies of the document and the Primary Source Close-Up graphic organizer (page 29) and distribute them to students.

If possible, provide the historical context for the primary source document and help students fill in the top section of the organizer. (Remind students that such information is not always available and may have to be investigated through other sources or deduced from the document.) Invite students to study the document carefully and describe exactly what they observe. Have them record their observations in the left lens of the eyeglasses on the graphic organizer.

Encourage students to ask questions about elements that seem important or unusual, such as the quality of a photograph, the style of writing, or references to devices that are no longer used. The more details students can ask questions about, the richer their analysis will be. Instruct students to complete the right lens with their reflections about what these details show.

Individually or in pairs, ask students to consider both the document's historical context and their reflections to fill in the document purpose. If there is a stated purpose in the document, have them consider another reason the document might have been created or an effect the document may have had.

Ask students: *How dependable do you think this source is? Would you recommend this source to another student studying your topic?* Have students rank the document on a scale of 1 to 10—10 being most dependable—and require them to support their reasons (e.g., details of a scene from a day-after account by an eyewitness might rank higher than a memoir entry from an eyewitness remembering the same event from a distance of forty years).

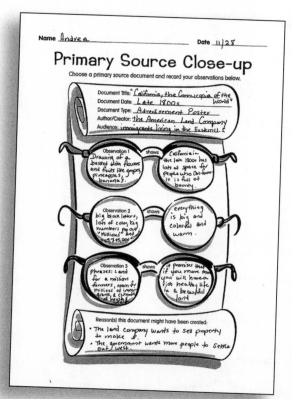

Primary Source Close-Up

Choose a primary source document and record your observations below.

Document Title: _____

Document Date: _____

Document Type: _____

Author/Creator: _____

Audience: _____

Observation 1   shows

Observation 2   shows

Observation 3   shows

Reason(s) this document might have been created:

On the Historical Fiction Trail

Skills

- Reads and responds to historical fiction

- Identifies key literary elements: setting, character, and plot

- Distinguishes between historical fact and fiction

Purpose

While students often like to read historical fiction, they also tend to have difficulty sorting fact from fiction and understanding an author's bias. This organizer offers students a way to keep track of the literary elements of a historical fiction novel. A completed organizer can serve as a guide for writing a full report on the book that includes a summary and an analysis of how the book presented the setting and characters and followed the events of a given time period.

How to Use the Organizer

Discuss with the class the elements of historical fiction. Your discussion might highlight areas that can be confusing for students. Explain that historical fiction is based on a historical event or person, yet it may include fictional events when there is no record of what happened. It also may feature fictional characters that help drive the plot and provide perspectives on the event that we may not be able to understand through primary sources. You might point out that authors of historical fiction often handpick and highlight certain events and characters while leaving out others to make their story more coherent.

Have students select a historical fiction novel related to your unit of study and leveled appropriately for their reading abilities. When students have selected their novel, distribute copies of the On the Historical Fiction Trail graphic organizer (page 31). As students read, have them complete the organizer by chapters or sections of the book, filling in the chapter or page numbers for each section they have read. Provide as many copies of the organizer as students need.

For each completed chapter or section, have students fill in the character and event sections in the wagons. Tell them to focus on only a few key events and characters. Students keep track of historical accuracy by sorting the characters and events in the Historical and Fictional wagons. They may need to use the author's notes, an online search engine, textbook, encyclopedia, or other sources to check whether the character existed or the event actually happened.

More to Do

Have students write a book report on their historical fiction novel. Encourage them to discuss the purposes key fictional characters served and the choices about fictional events the author made.

On the Historical Fiction Trail

Compare fact with fiction as you read a historical fiction piece. Record the characters and events as they appear in history and in fiction.

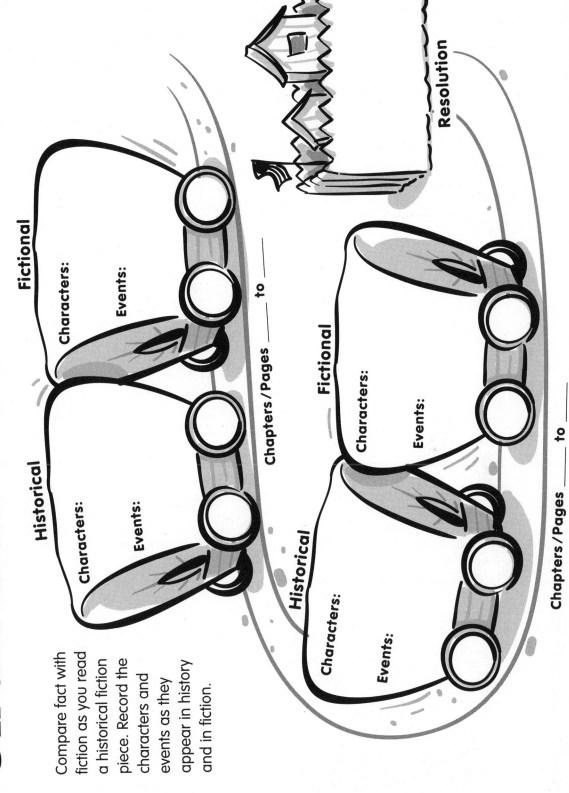

Fictional

Characters:

Events:

Historical

Characters:

Events:

Chapters / Pages ____ to ____

Resolution

Fictional

Characters:

Events:

Historical

Characters:

Events:

Chapters / Pages ____ to ____

Textbook Chapter Outliner

Skills

- Outlines a chapter of a textbook
- Uses key nonfiction elements to support comprehension
- Synthesizes important information

Purpose

The practice of outlining a textbook chapter not only helps students retain key concepts and important details for end-of-chapter tests, but also builds a historical framework in their minds. Using the outline organizer as a guide during reading is one way to keep students focused on the chapter's main ideas and to help them navigate the textbook more efficiently.

How to Use the Organizer

One of the most important things we can teach students is how to use their textbook as a learning tool. Before you introduce this organizer, walk students through a chapter of their textbook, thinking aloud about how you read to learn. Point out that you can reduce reading time and quickly understand the main idea(s) of the chapter by previewing the chapter. Invite students to make predictions about what they'll learn based on the chapter title and subheads, help them notice key terms in boldface, and encourage them to look carefully at maps, illustrations, and other visual aids and to read the captions.

Distribute copies of the Textbook Chapter Outliner graphic organizer (page 33). Display a transparency copy of the organizer on the overhead projector, and begin to structure the chapter outline with student input. Enlist their help filling in the organizer with the chapter title and subtitles (in the order they appear).

Then have them read the first section of the chapter and pull out two or three important details, noting any important terms that support those details. Guide students to fill in the first row of the organizer with this information. Make sure that they use brief notes in the "Important Details" space and avoid adding notes that don't directly support the main idea. Fill in the transparency as students give their responses and instruct them to fill in their own copies. Provide students with additional copies of the organizer as needed.

More to Do

When students can outline a chapter well, encourage them to try the next chapter in pairs or individually. To reinforce the process of outlining a textbook chapter and to transfer nonfiction reading skills in other subject areas, consider having students use this organizer to outline a chapter from their science, health, or any other content-area textbook.

Textbook Chapter Outliner

Fill in this graphic organizer to help you keep track of
key concepts and details in your textbook.

Chapter Title: _____

Subhead	Important Details	Key Terms
1. _____ Main Idea:		
2. _____ Main Idea:		
3. _____ Main Idea:		
4. _____ Main Idea:		
5. _____ Main Idea:		

1-2-3 Summary

Skills

- Synthesizes main ideas from a news article or nonfiction passage

- Records background knowledge and new understandings about the reading

- Organizes ideas for a summary paragraph

Purpose

When we ask students to read and summarize an article or passage about a current or historical event, we want them to be able to give more than a cursory outline; we want them to be able to present an overview of the reading and place it within their own schema—what they knew before and what interested them about the reading. This organizer offers a simple format in which students can show that they comprehend the whole of what they've read. You can use students' completed organizers as a tool for evaluating basic comprehension.

How to Use the Organizer

Encourage students who need more support with summary writing to use the organizer in three stages: before, during, and after reading. Distribute copies of the 1-2-3 Summary graphic organizer (page 35) and the article students will read and summarize. Have students read the title, skim the article, and fill in space number 1 on the organizer to access prior knowledge.

While students are reading, instruct them to flag or highlight important ideas in their article. After they've finished reading, have them identify three or four main ideas, completing space number 2. If the article is in a narrative or chronological format, have students fill in the short lines with sequence transition words, such as *first, second, third,* and *finally,* to help them organize chronologically.

Have students also find a fact or idea from the article that amazed or interested them and fill in space number 3.

To help students write their summary paragraph, give them a summary frame into which they can insert the ideas they recorded in the organizer:

Before I read about [topic], I knew [section 1 ideas]. In [article title] I learned [section 2 ideas]. I was amazed to find out [section 3 ideas].

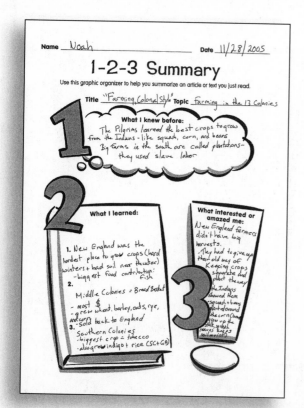

1-2-3 Summary

Use this graphic organizer to help you summarize an article or text you just read.

Title _____

What I knew before reading:

What I learned:

What interested or amazed me:

Triple-Decker Essay Planner

Skills

- Develops a position on a historical event or current issue

- Selects three reasons to support the position

- Gives three details from research to support each reason

- Organizes the argument for a five-paragraph persuasive essay

Purpose

The Triple-Decker Essay Planner graphic organizer helps students generate and structure a well-developed argument for a position they will take on a historical or current issue. They may use it as a prewriting tool not only for persuasive essays, but also for expository essays.

How to Use the Organizer

If students have not written essays before, have the class read a well-constructed five-paragraph essay, such as an op-ed piece with a central argument and at least three main points that provide supporting details for the argument. Display a transparency copy of the Triple-Decker Essay Planner graphic organizer (page 37) on the overhead projector. Then work backward, filling in the organizer as students identify each part of the essay: the introductory paragraph with the position statement (the top bun shape), the main points (the three oval burger shapes), the supporting details for each main point (the three thick cheese rectangles), and the conclusion (the bottom bun shape).

Let students pick from several current or historical issues they have studied and develop position questions, such as: *What was the most important technological advance of the twentieth century in America?* or *Should kids younger than 15 years old be allowed to work?* Distribute copies of the graphic organizer. Have students work individually, in pairs, or in small groups to complete the organizer. Encourage them to refer back to the sources they used to find supporting details for their arguments.

When students have completed their organizers satisfactorily, have them use the triple-decker framework as a guide to write their persuasive essays: The notes in the top bun form the introductory paragraph with the position statement, the notes in each burger/cheese pair become a supporting paragraph with a reason and evidence, and the notes in the bottom bun become the conclusion.

More to Do

To adapt this organizer for planning an expository essay, have students develop a thesis on a historical topic. Remind them to follow the framework as they would for the persuasive essay, stating a thesis rather than a position, and giving main points rather than arguments.

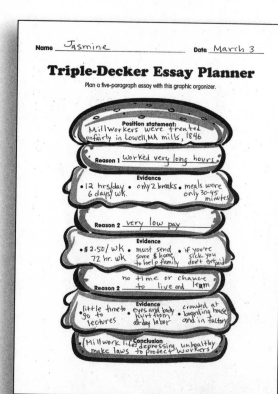

Triple-Decker Essay Planner

Plan a five-paragraph essay with this graphic organizer.

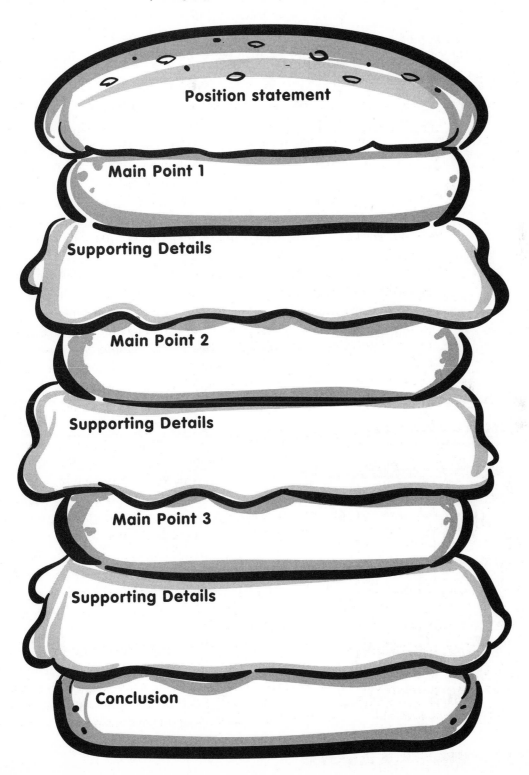

Position statement

Main Point 1

Supporting Details

Main Point 2

Supporting Details

Main Point 3

Supporting Details

Conclusion

All My Sources

Skills

- Identifies sources available for a research project
- Distinguishes among types of sources
- Evaluates uses for each source

Purpose

This basic planner helps students who are just beginning their research to identify a variety of sources they might use for a project. For students with more sophisticated research skills, this organizer supports their planning process, helping them show how they will use each of the sources they have identified.

How to Use the Organizer

For students new to research, take some time to explore different types of sources, including encyclopedia articles, textbooks, nonfiction books and articles, online sources, audiovisual sources, and primary sources (see the "Primary Sources Close-Up" lesson on page 28 for tips on locating primary sources online). When students have selected a research topic, distribute copies of the All My Sources graphic organizer (page 39) and have them fill in each source's title and any other bibliographical data or location notes you want them to record.

The completed organizer can serve as an accountability tool while students conduct and prepare to present their research: Have students keep their organizer nearby for reference and encourage them to make notes on it about the sources they use. This could be as simple as having students mark a check-plus (√+) next to a source title to show that they took and used notes from that source for their research. Or they might take more detailed notes by placing a sticky note next to a source title with comments about how useful the source was for answering their research question or how difficult it was to use.

You might also design a scoring rubric that includes the criteria of how many and what types of sources students are expected to use. Students can make sure they have met the criteria by using the organizer to keep track of the sources they've found and used.

More to Do

Students who are ready for more challenging work may note what aspects of their research topic the source covers or what questions they might answer with the help of this source. For example, students learning about the Civil War might list letters home from Union and Confederate soldiers in the "Primary Sources" space on the organizer and note that these sources will give them information about the life of a soldier fighting in the Civil War.

All My Sources

As you conduct research, list and organize your sources in this chart.

Topic _____

Sources Matrix

Skills

- Collects information from a variety of sources

- Classifies types of information sources

- Distinguishes between primary and secondary sources

Purpose

The sources matrix offers a tool for students to record and sort reference sources as they collect information about a research topic. The matrix prepares them to cite the sources they will use in a written or oral report and check that they have used a variety of types.

How to Use the Organizer

If students need support with selecting sources, determine the number and types of sources students will use for a particular project (for example, students will use one original source, one encyclopedia entry, one nonfiction book, and one Web site for their reports). Make a copy of the Sources Matrix graphic organizer (page 41) and fill in the column heads with the selected types of sources. Then make copies of this page and distribute them to the class. If students are expected to generate the number and types of sources themselves, or if you wish to differentiate the assignment for individual students, leave the matrix blank, make copies, and distribute. Then work with each student to set an appropriate goal.

As students collect sources, have them fill in the titles in the far-left column. In the box located at the intersection of the source type and source title, encourage students to either mark a check (√) when they have used the source or write the date(s) on which they've taken notes from that source. Have students use the far-right column in one of the following ways: to collect full bibliographical data on the source, make notes on the source (for example, topics covered, usefulness), or distinguish it as a primary or secondary source.

Name _Sergio_   Date _1/28_

Sources Matrix

Record your sources in this matrix, under the appropriate type and jot down notes in the last column.

Topic: _Chinese laborers and the Gold Rush_

Sources	Type Primary Source	Type Article	Type Encyclopedia	Type Book	Notes
"Chinese Transformed 'Gold Mountain'"	.	√ 3/5			www.goldrush.com/index.html Tells about pay, types of work, prejudices
"1848-1850: A Timeline"		√ 3/5			Textbook- Chapt. 5 Immigration dates and population numbers in California.
"Western Frontier Life in America"			√ 3/7		www.textbookonline.com/mb/Article?id=or59900 Struggles and jobs for immigrants
The California Gold Rush by R. Conrad Stein				√ 3/8	How different groups got along, worked together, made their way
"The Magic Washer"	√ 3/9				Washing detergent ad from 1886 promises to do such a good job people won't need Chinese workers to wash their clothes.

Sources Matrix

Record your sources in this matrix under the appropriate type and jot down notes in the last column.

Topic: _____

Sources	Type	Type	Type	Type	Notes

Inquiry Chart

Skills

- Generates questions to guide research

- Uses multiple sources to locate answers to questions

- Identifies conflicting information

Purpose

The Inquiry Chart (developed by Hoffman, 1992) challenges students to develop interest-based questions that will help them conduct research on a topic. To find the answers to their questions and fill in the chart, students must take notes from multiple sources. This process helps them confirm answers when sources agree and identify inconsistencies among the sources when there are differences in information—a jumping-off point for comparing the validity of the sources.

How to Use the Organizer

Use this advanced organizer with individual students or with small groups of students who are interested in the same topic. Be sure to model for students how to generate good questions and complete the I-chart using a topic and sources with which students are familiar.

When students have selected and previewed at least three sources for their research topic, distribute copies of the Inquiry Chart graphic organizer (page 43) and ask them to write the source titles in the boxes of the first column. Then have students generate three questions related to the topic. Encourage them to think of big ideas they want to learn about and to develop questions, such as: *Why did so many immigrants come from Europe a hundred years ago?* Also encourage them to speculate about conflicting information they may have heard about the topic. This might include disparate dates for a single event or even different causes for an event. Guide them to write their questions in the first row of the chart in the columns labeled "Question."

As they read, have students use the organizer to record information that answers each question in the box located at the intersection of the focus question and the source from which they located the information. Explain that knowing where each piece of information came from really helps researchers share information and learn which sources they can trust. Have students mark a check (√) next to information that is confirmed by two or more sources and highlight conflicting information among the sources.

After reviewing the information in each column, have students write at the bottom of the column a one-sentence summary that synthesizes their learning or evaluates the sources.

Inquiry Chart

Decide on three questions to help focus
your research. Use this chart to record
answers from different sources.

Topic:

	Question	Question	Question
Source 1			
Source 2			
Source 3			
Comments			

SMART Presentation Planner

Skills

- Chooses the form, content, and style for a presentation on a historical event or figure

- Organizes a presentation for a specific audience

- Selects an effective presentation "voice"

Purpose

This planner helps students complete the first stage of planning for a presentation. It is particularly helpful for students who have never given a presentation before or who are just learning about how to present to a specific audience. It also supports students' understanding of point of view by allowing them to deliver the presentation in the role of a character who is familiar with the event or figure they've studied.

How to Use the Organizer

When students have selected a subject or you have given them a list of choices for an end-of-unit presentation, have the class brainstorm ideas for presentation formats they would enjoy (for example, TV or radio news reports, one-act plays, PowerPoint slide shows) and the related roles they might play as presenter (for example, journalist, historical figure, eyewitness to an event).

Distribute copies of the SMART Presentation Planner (page 45) to students so they can use the planner to shape their "SMART" presentation. Let them fill in the subject, type of presentation, and role they've chosen in the appropriate spaces on the organizer. Instruct them to record any materials they'll need in the "Type of Presentation" space. To encourage students to develop a strong voice for the role they've selected, give them time to share ideas with classmates as to what their characters might say about their chosen subjects. Ask them to write in the "Role" space some phrases they can imagine saying in this role.

Then have them fill in the "Audience" space of the organizer, naming their target audience (peers, parents, or a historical audience) and what the audience will want to know. Finally, with all of this information, have students fill in the "Main Idea" space with the key idea(s) that they want to communicate to their audience.

Students can use their organizers to focus the written part of their presentation, returning to the organizer for reminders about the voice they are using to deliver the presentation, the audience to whom they are speaking, the format of the presentation, and the key ideas they wish to present.

SMART Presentation Planner

Plan your presentation with this graphic organizer.

Audience

Subject

Main Ideas

Type of Presentation

Role

It's Show Time!

Skills

- Takes notes for a presentation on a historical subject

- Organizes the information by importance

- Plans within a given time frame

Purpose

This planning guide provides a simple structure in which students place key ideas in order of importance and allot an appropriate amount of time for each part of their oral presentation. Used in tandem with a stopwatch, it becomes a useful tool for improving students' ability to speak publicly with confidence—practicing from the planner notes can help them decide to condense or lengthen the speech and improve their ability to pace themselves.

How to Use the Organizer

When students have selected the presentation topic and had time to consider how they will creatively deliver the topic (see the "SMART Presentation Planner," page 44), distribute copies of the It's Show Time! graphic organizer (page 47).

Tell students the total time allotted for their presentation and have them write that number in the "Total Time" box on the organizer. Explain that they may divide up the time among each area of the presentation as they see fit (for example, they may allow extra time for their strongest point). Or you may want to dictate more structured time constraints.

Have students consider the order of their oral presentation: Which of their three main points is the strongest or most interesting, and at what point would it make the biggest splash—at the beginning or end? Encourage students to be brief as they fill in notes for each part of their presentation in the dialogue bubble shapes. The words they write should serve as reminders about what they'll say rather than as a script. (If students need a script, let them write out the script on index cards.)

After students have outlined what they will say and set the time limits for each part, instruct them to note any set-up reminders and list materials they'll need in the box at the top of the organizer. As they review their speech notes, they can add tips to the "Notes" boxes.

Before the oral presentation, let students practice at least once with a partner. Assign one partner to present and the other to follow along on the presenter's organizer and keep track of time. Then have partners switch roles. When students run significantly over or under the time limit, have them add or cut material so that they can present successfully within the parameters.

Name ______________________________ Date ______________

It's Show Time!

Plan your oral presentation with this graphic organizer.
Use the Time clocks at the right to help pace yourself.

Setup Notes/Materials → TIME ___ : ___

Intro — NOTES → ___ : ___

Main point 1 — NOTES → ___ : ___

Main point 2 — NOTES → ___ : ___

Main point 3 — NOTES → ___ : ___

Conclusion — NOTES → ___ : ___

TOTAL TIME ___ : ___

Bibliography

Bromley, K., L. Irwin-De Vitis & M. Modlo. (1995). *Graphic Organizers: Visual Strategies for Active Learning.* New York: Scholastic Inc.

Boyle, J.R. & M. Weishaar. (1997). "The Effects of Expert-Generated Versus Student-Generated Cognitive Organizers on the Reading Comprehension of Students with Learning Disabilities." *Learning Disabilities Research and Practice,* 12(4), 228–235.

Chang, K.E., Y.T. Sung & I.D. Chen. (2002). "The Effect of Concept Mapping to Enhance Text Comprehension and Summarization." *Journal of Experimental Education,* 71(1), 5–24.

Dodge, J. (2005). *Differentiation in Action.* New York: Scholastic Inc.

Ellis, E.S. (1994). "Integrating Writing Instruction with Content-Area Instruction: Part II: Writing Processes." *Intervention in School and Clinic,* 29(4), 219–230.

Guastello, E.F. (2000). "Concept Mapping Effects on Science Content Comprehension of Low-Achieving Inner-City Seventh Graders." *Remedial and Special Education,* 21(6), 356.

Hoffman, J. (1992). "Critical Reading/Thinking Across the Curriculum: Using I-charts to Support Learning." *Language Arts,* 69, 121–127.

Moore, D. & J. Readence. (1984). "A Quantitative and Qualitative Review of Graphic Organizer Research." *Journal of Educational Research,* 78(1), 11–17.

National Center on Accessing the General Curriculum. (2002). http://www.cast.org/index.html